SECRETS OF THE CONFIDENT SPEAKER:
MASTERING THE INNER GAME OF PUBLIC SPEAKING

WHAT EXPERTS ARE SAYING ABOUT
JONATHAN LI

"If you follow Jonathan Li's advice, you'll be able to conquer your fear of public speaking and take the stage with confidence."

—**DR. NICK MORGAN,** author of *Power Cues: The Subtle Science of Leading Groups, Persuading Others, and Maximizing Your Personal Impact*

"Jonathan Li is one of the most expressive leaders in the business world."

— **TJ WALKER,** *Wall Street Journal* best-selling author of *TJ Walker's Secret to Foolproof Presentations*

"Jonathan's new book will save you time and money! *Secrets of the Confident Speaker* is helpful, honest, informative, and well organized. The advice Jonathan shares is essential for your public speaking and business success."

— **AKASH KARIA,** *Amazon* best-selling author of *How to Deliver a Great TED Talk*

"Nothing will increase your level of success as much as being comfortable presenting your ideas in public. In this excellent step-by-step guide, Jonathan Li helps you understand that becoming a confident speaker is easier than you think. It is just a matter of taking the steps he has outlined in his book."

— **PATRICIA FRIPP,** Hall of Fame speaker

"Jonathan Li's book will give you lots to think about when it comes to speaking, and also when it comes to business itself.
Dig in and learn."

— **CHRIS BROGAN,** *New York Times* best-selling author of *Trust Agents: Using the Web to Build Influence, Improve Reputation, and Earn Trust*

WHAT PAST CLIENTS ARE SAYING ABOUT JONATHAN LI

"AMAZING! I just started getting coaching from Jonathan Li on how to overcome your fears and challenges when it comes to public speaking and how to deliver a winning public speaking talk, and he completely blew me out of the water in our first session! This guy is a public speaking Jedi master and has delivered a TEDx talk, so he has the experience to back up his methods. If you ever have to do public speaking and have some fears around it, or just want to up your game to the next level, you should check him out!"
— PHIL MACNEVIN

"Jonathan gives me confidence. When I use what Jonathan taught me and relate my talking points to daily life, it is easier for people to get my ideas. "
— ENZO CHIU

"Jonathan helped me overcome my nervousness with public speaking and deliver my talk with confidence. So grateful for his advice – Jonathan is amazing!"
— KATE ERICKSON

DEDICATION

TO MY MUM, DAD, AND SISTER.

For believing in me and in my work.

CONTENTS

INTRODUCTION:
WHY YOU SHOULD READ THIS BOOK

I am passionate about helping you feel comfortable and confident speaking in front of groups. As a coach, my goal is to make sure that you always look good in front of your boss, team, and clients. To achieve that goal, I have compiled some of the most effective techniques I use in my coaching practice and my speaking career. Additionally, I have interviewed some of the world's greatest speakers. Within the pages of this book, you will find their tips and secrets to being the best public speaker possible.

I know what it takes to develop a strong speaking ability, the kind that wins over the crowd, impresses the boss, or secures a sale because I've been through it myself. While I have spent more than six years coaching others to overcome their fear and confidently take the stage, I didn't start out that way.

For years my mind would blank the moment I was on stage. I would say "um" or pause for too long all the time. I would move around nervously and awkwardly. My voice would shake, or I would speak too softly. I certainly didn't impress anyone. The fear of public speaking was hurting my career and holding me back.

I had to take action to improve my speaking. So I focused on learning from the best and figuring out the most effective ways to become a confident public speaker. By using the practical skills included in this book, I was qualified to give a TEDx talk. I've been featured on *The Huffington Post*, *Lifehack* and *Business Insider*. Now, when I speak, I impress my boss, team, and clients.

I've condensed that expertise into this short and readable guide. I understand you are busy—who has time to read 300 pages? This powerful book gets to the point: you'll discover the secrets to becoming a confident speaker in minutes. Carry it with you. When you need to deliver a message, read it. The techniques you learn here will help you feel comfortable and confident speaking in public.

We'll begin with the three simple steps that form the foundation of confident speaking:

PREPARE ⇨ PRACTICE ⇨ PERFORM

- **Structure**
- **Slides**

- **Voice**
- **Video**
- **Q&A**

We'll be covering each of the steps in depth in this book and learning about the following:

Prepare

- The Quick Talk technique I use to prepare a great speech or presentation in just minutes.

- The Magic Switch technique I use to stop worrying about what others think of me and start speaking with confidence.

- The exact script you can use to open a speech or presentation so that you will grab the audience's attention immediately.

- The most effective way to close your speech or presentation – and the best way to inspire your audience to take action.

- The Simple Story Quadrant you can use to connect with your audience emotionally every time.

Practice

- Eight ways to make your voice louder and stronger today.

- The secret weapon that I use (and other people ignore) to make my voice louder and clearer.

- The Simple Practice Method I use to improve my speaking skills quickly.

- Why practice doesn't make perfect – and why many people who practice a lot don't remember what to say.

- Why you don't have to memorize your talk word-for-word to remember what you want to say.

Perform

- The Public Speaking Success Ritual you can use to feel comfortable and confident speaking in public.

- One thing you can do before your talk to show the audience you care about them and win their support. (This is crucial for your public speaking success!)

I hope you enjoy this book. I can't wait to hear how it increased your confidence, helped you to stand out in the workplace, and transformed your feelings about public speaking. If you'd like to get in touch and share your story, reach me at
TheRealJonathanLi@gmail.com

UNDERSTANDING YOUR FEAR OF PUBLIC SPEAKING: HOW TO STOP WORRYING AND START SPEAKING

I was a nervous speaker for years. My fear of public speaking was so severe that it was hurting my career and holding me back.

On top of the impact that my fear was having on my job, it felt terrible. Everyone was looking at me. I was sweating. My voice was shaking. I always worried that the people in the crowd thought I was stupid. I felt like a loser.

Even worse, I was forced to deliver talks regularly. It was a key part of my job. I knew I had a lot to lose if I didn't solve my problem. But I also had a lot to gain if I did. The ability to speak well in public comes with many benefits, including success or the appearance of being highly successful, smart, and great at what I do.

Why Public Speaking Is Linked To Being Successful

Speaking with confidence allows you to:

A. Look good in front of your boss, team, and clients.

B. Make more money.

C. Influence others and get what you want.

These are great outcomes! Still, incentives (no matter how great they may sound) can only go so far in helping you overcome a fear that is, in a manner of speaking, hardwired into your brain.

Why We Still Fear of Public Speaking

If you were to face the angry lion above, your brain would snap into survival mode: *It's gonna eat me! Run!*

Your brain's approach to fear and survival is built-in – and when we're talking about avoiding a lion attack, that is a great thing. Unfortunately, your brain has only one reaction to fear stimuli, and it will deploy it when necessary whether the trigger is a hungry lion or a waiting audience.

When giving a presentation, you may be thinking this same thing: *They're gonna hate me! Run!*

Public speaking is scary because it means you might fail or be rejected by the group. In some cases – like when I was struggling with this fear – your brain might start telling you those things will happen before you even get started: "Everyone judges me. They must think I'm stupid. I'm embarrassing myself." Once your brain goes down that path, it can be difficult to muster the confidence needed to give a good performance.

Is It True That The Fear Never Goes Away?

I'm afraid so. The fear doesn't go away because our brains are wired to help us survive. Given that this wiring lives in the oldest part of our brains, changing it is not really possible. Besides, we'll want those mechanisms in place if we face a lion.

You may be surprised to know that those same fear reactions are likely to show up for just about everyone. After all, even the best speakers have the same wiring in their brains. Mark Twain, one of the smartest people ever lived, said, "There are two types of speakers: those that are nervous and those that are liars."

So, there's no way to get rid of the fear entirely, but we can control it and put it to work for us. In fact, fear can be a good thing.

Use The Magic Switch Technique To Stop Worrying And Start Speaking With Confidence

Having a little fear is helpful because it motivates you to succeed. The fear gives you the energy to prevent failures. The fear drives you to work hard to avoid looking stupid in front of the audience. You do your best to impress.

Just like excitement, nervousness creates energy. The body can't tell the difference. Don't use the energy to hurt you; use it to help you.

Instead of focusing on yourself, focus on the audience.

Switch your focus with The Magic Switch Technique:

> Imagine speaking in front of a group. Are you worrying about what people think about you? Take a moment to notice that fear. Don't worry, it won't be staying long.

> Snap your finger. (Yes, really do it.)

> With the snap, switch the focus from yourself to your audience. Remind yourself, "I don't let my fear hold me back. I focus on serving the audience." How will your talk help or serve the people in the crowd? You are about to bring something positive to them. Focus on doing that!

The Magic Switch Technique was a big breakthrough for me in my early efforts to conquer my fear. By shifting my focus outward, I got out of my head. The fearful voice that told me I would fail started to diminish. Instead, I saw opportunities for how I could serve my audience even better by explaining my talking points clearly or by answering questions.

The fear still appears every now and then, but I put it to work for me.

PREPARATION MADE SIMPLE: HOW TO GET ATTENTION, CONNECT WITH YOUR AUDIENCE, AND INSPIRE ACTION

Before I became an expert on public speaking, I never wanted to prepare for a talk. I preferred just to wing it, justifying my decision by saying, "I'm so busy! It's a waste of my time! I'll be fine!" Of course, once it was time to give the talk, I didn't know what to say. The talk would be terrible and the audience would hate me.

There's no shortcut to preparing a talk. Skip it at your own risk. BUT that doesn't mean you need to spend days slaving over it. With a clear structure, you can prepare a talk in minutes.

I worked with a very well known speaking coach. (I choose not to use her name because I want to maintain our good relationship.) One key point I got from my work with her is that you have to create a clear message. The way she said it was:

> "If you had one sentence instead of the entire talk, what would you say?"

I have created my own variation of that question in my work with clients. It cuts to the heart of the preparation process and creates the foundation of any great talk. That's why it is the first of five key pieces of my Quick Talk Technique.

The Quick Talk Technique – Five Secrets For Preparing The Perfect Talk In Just Minutes

While preparing for my TEDx talk *How To Speak With Confidence*, I created The Quick Talk Technique. This method requires that you go through the following five steps to create a winning presentation.

1. Message

Finding your answer is an essential first step, since it will decide what you include in your talk. The clearer your message is, the easier it will be to build your speech around it. So that's where we'll start.

To create a powerful message, ask:

> "What do I want the audience to think, feel or do
> *differently* after my talk?"

In my TEDx talk, the message was, "Everyone can learn how to speak with confidence." What I wanted them to *think differently* was that everyone could become a confident public speaker.

From there, decide what will stay and what will go by asking: "Will this part make them think, feel or do *differently?* If something contributes to your aim, include it in your talk. If not, throw it away.

2. Brainstorming

List out all of the points that you've decided will support your message. Next, organize them into a logical order (e.g., "Step One, Step Two, Step Three," order of importance, or timeline).

Choose, at most, three main points that support your message. In his book *Rhetoric,* Aristotle wrote about the rule of three: People tend to remember three things easily. The chances are that people will only remember three points from your talk. Plan in advance what these points will be.

The three points in my TEDx talk were: Prepare. Practice. Perform.

3. Opening

People now seem to have a shorter attention span than a goldfish. They decide whether they should listen to you in eight seconds, according to Microsoft. If you fail to grab their attention, you will lose them. Open strong. Make sure you catch the audience's attention within eight seconds.

Here are three ways to create a strong opening:

A. Say Nothing

Pause. Just smile and scan your audience. The speaker who is comfortable with silence commands attention. People will look up, and they will pay attention to you.

B. Share a Story the Audience Will Care About

In *The Story Factor,* Annette Simmons writes, "Influence is a function of grabbing someone's attention, connecting to what they already feel is important, and linking that feeling to whatever you want them to see, do or feel." By opening with a story you know the audience can relate to or value, you will capture their attention immediately.

C. Ask a Rhetorical Question

Your audience will want to know the answer.

While I started my TEDx talk with a personal story, the easiest way to grab attention is to ask a rhetorical question. When you ask a question and then answer it yourself, people won't interrupt you, and you take control.

Let's say you're preparing a talk about effective public speaking. Here's a word-for-word script you can use to grab the audience's attention immediately:

> *If I ask you, "Do you want to stand on stage and speak with confidence?"*
>
> *Maybe you'll say "yes."*
>
> *Maybe "no."*
>
> *Most likely, you'll say, "Yes, can you show me how?"*
>
> *In the next few minutes, you will discover three simple steps on how to become a confident speaker.*
>
> *Let's start with step one...*

This opening will grab your audience's attention and allow you to hold it throughout your talk.

4. Stories

Stories help you connect with the audience emotionally. They also help you remember points more effectively. Instead of memorizing logical reasons or endless scripts, tell stories.

When you remember the story, you remember the point. Our brains are hardwired to receive information in that way. Telling a story ensures your audience will pay attention and remember what you say.

The best stories you can tell are personal stories. They help connect with your audience emotionally. People will pay more attention and remember you because they connect you with the story. Also, it's better to tell your own story than it is to talk about someone else. For one thing, no one can tell your story better than you. Added bonus: you'll remember what to say because you have probably told it to friends before.

The audience wants to hear your story. When you share your own struggles and inspire people, you're saying, "Hey, come and connect with me." Your audience members will see themselves in your story because you have built an emotional connection. When they can see themselves in your story, they can also see themselves in your solution. Then you're not just someone who did it; you're a guide who can show them how to do it too.

The Simple Story Quadrant – Never Tell A Story Without This Tool

If you dive into the world of storytelling, you will know Joseph Campbell, author of *The Hero with a Thousand Faces*. He is famous for The Hero's Journey, a tough storytelling pattern with over twelve stages, ranging from "Ordinary World" to "Call To Adventure" and "Crossing the Threshold." The formula is built for myths, not real-life stories. That's why even professional writers find it difficult.

By simplifying The Hero's Journey and other popular storytelling formulas, I have developed The Simple Story Quadrant. By using this model, you can easily create a compelling story and connect with your audience emotionally every time.

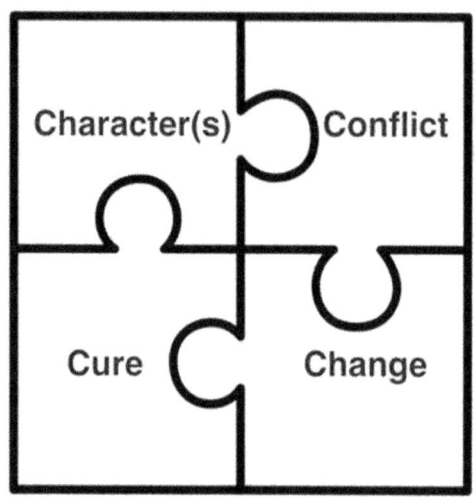

Let's take a closer look at each component.

Character(s)

The main character in your story has to have a connection to your audience members. Imagine that you need to introduce yourself to a group of executives, what story would you tell? Who would the main character be? Would those executives be more likely to pay attention to a struggling college graduate trying to find his first job, or a struggling executive trying to increase profits?

For example, if I were to step up in front of a crowd of people who wanted to speak with confidence, I could share a story of *me being a nervous speaker*.

Find what your audience members are interested in, so you can easily connect with them. Maybe you both face a common challenge. Share it so the audience will connect with you.

When the audience can relate to your main character, they will pay more attention to you, thinking, "Wow, this person is just like me. Maybe I can apply this lesson in my life," or, "If he can do it, so can I!"

Conflict

Tension makes your story interesting. The conflict grabs the audience's attention because it makes people think, "I wonder what will happen next." Your audience members can relate to the struggles and connect with you. Here are three kinds of conflict you can use:

> *You versus others.* You're fighting your enemy. Your struggling businessman's competitor is eating up the market share. This is effective because your audience loves watching good people fighting villains. A story with a villain is fun to listen to. Think Hollywood action movies.

> *You versus the environment.* You're fighting external forces beyond your control. The economy is so bad that the struggling executive doesn't know what to do. It is exciting to see a human fighting something bigger than himself. Excited, your audience will think, "I wonder how this will end."

> *You versus yourself.* You're fighting internal forces like fear. Your struggling executive is beginning to doubt his ability to

achieve his goal. It's a safe bet that your audience will recognize and relate to elements of this internal fight.

Here's the conflict I would use in a "speak with confidence" talk:

For years while being forced to speak in front of groups, my mind would go blank. I would say um all the time. The fear of public speaking was hurting my career and holding me back.

Share your failures because they make you human. While the audience expects you to brag about your successes, do the opposite. People will think, "I can relate to the speaker. Let me pay attention and see what will happen next." You will have their full attention.

Cure

The cure can be an expert or a life-changing experience. An expert says something that inspires the struggling executive to overcome the conflict. Or it can be an experience that teaches the main character something new.

Use dialogue when delivering the solution. World Champion Speaker Craig Valentine is a master of dialogue who said, "Speaking is a dialogue and not a monologue." Use dialogue because it breathes life into your story and makes you audience feel they are in the story with you. Doing so will make them pay attention to your story.

Here's my "speak with confidence" cure:

I said to myself, "I must learn from the best speakers in the world."

Change

Show how the Cure now changes the character's life for the better. The executive is no longer struggling. The fearful speaker is now confident. Use detail and show a real picture of what the change looks like and how good it feels.

My "speak with confidence" change is:

> *I discovered the real secrets on how to become a confident public speaker. By using these practical skills, I was qualified to give a TEDx talk. I've been featured on The Huffington Post, Lifehack and Business Insider. Now, when I speak, I impress my boss, team, and clients."*

When people see that the Cure (advice or lesson) delivers the benefits they want, they will be more motivated to take action.

5. Closing

Summarize your points so people will remember what you said and take action. Give them a clear action step, so they know what to do next.

The script I use to inspire my audience to take action is:

> *So how do we become a confident public speaker?*
>
> *Simply give your name, email, and you'll receive instant access to free training on how to speak with confidence.*
>
> *Thanks for listening and I'll talk to you soon.*

Another example is the ending of my TEDx talk:

> *So how do we speak with confidence?*
>
> *Prepare. Practice. Perform.*
>
> *Here's my challenge for you: Follow these three simple steps so that you too can speak with confidence.*

With The Quick Talk Technique and The Simple Story Quadrant, I prepared my TEDx talk in minutes. That speech was stronger than any I had done before. Use it, and you will prepare your talk in minutes.

COMMUNICATING VISUALLY: HOW TO MAKE A POWERPOINT PRESENTATION

I was so bored that I wanted to kill myself. I was sitting there, watching the speaker click through slides full of bullet points. His voice was boring, and the stream of information was monotonous. I had stopped taking notes twenty minutes ago. I was thinking dinner.

That afternoon was a textbook example of how NOT to do a presentation. If the speaker had followed The Professional Slides Method outlined below to communicate his message visually, his presentation would have been much better.

The Professional Slides Method – Hold Your Audience's Attention

You don't have to be a designer to make professional looking slides. Level up your presentation with The Professional Slides Method:

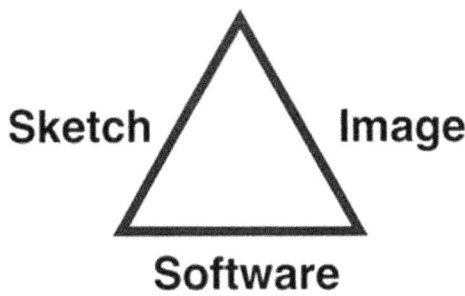

Let's examine the model, piece by piece.

Sketch

Use sticky notes to sketch your ideas visually, writing one idea on each note or "slide." You can use as many slides as you want, provided that they connect directly to your message.

Lay out the notes in the order you think they best fit and make sure they all connect in a logical way. This is a great way to catch any gaps in content or see if one piece doesn't fit with the rest.

At the end of this step, you will have the "bones" of your presentation.

Image

Much like our hungry lion in an earlier chapter, the image above creates a gut feeling because our brain is hardwired to respond to an attacking tiger. This threatening image snaps our brains to attention.

It also communicates with us on an intuitive level. I don't need to say words like "threatening" or "danger" because the tiger has already told you.

When you can find an image that creates this kind of emotional response, it's going to make a lasting impression.

Make sure you use images that create the strongest emotions possible. This tiger picture is a perfect example. I choose images that create strong emotions, whether I make people laugh, cry or just pay attention after being scared. When searching for images, I ask myself, "Does this image make me feel the way I want the audience to feel?" If you feel strong emotions, others will feel the same.

Be sure to use high-quality images. It's important, too, that you don't steal them. Don't go to Google Images because those images have copyrights. Go to stock image websites like Fotolia or Adobe Stock to find high-quality images at a reasonable price.

Software

Open up your favourite presentation software. Fill each slide with a full image that creates a strong emotion.

If you have to add keywords to the slide, add three words at most. Make sure people at the back can see the words clearly.

Use The Professional Slides Method for every talk and develop the skills and habits described in this book. Once you have mastered these skills, you will look good in front of your boss, team, and clients.

POWERFUL VOICE: HOW TO STOP YOUR VOICE FROM GETTING SHAKY (EVEN IF YOU ARE NERVOUS)

"Did you eat yet?" "Speak louder!"

I was losing them. I could tell my audience had stopped paying attention to what I was saying. My voice was shaking, and people in the back couldn't hear me. Clearly, they saw that I was nervous. Because of my voice, my presentation (and clearly my energy levels) seemed weak. It was my nightmare come to life.

After that terrible talk, I decided to find ways to strengthen my voice. I was then introduced to a celebrity voice coach named Roger Love, who has worked with Tony Robbins, Jennifer Lawrence, and Brendon Burchard. We did intensive voice training and exercises designed to make the vocal chords stronger. It was through my work with Roger Love that I learned the importance of warming up.

Just like a runner, a great speaker warms up before performing. Warm up your voice so that it will sound powerful, loud, and clear. Follow these steps to make sure your message gets heard.

Eight Ways To Make Your Voice Louder And Stronger Today

Your voice is like a muscle. The more you exercise your voice, the more powerful it becomes. When you have a loud and strong voice, people believe in you and your message.

Get Familiar With Your Voice

Your voice may sound perfectly normal to you when speaking. But when you listen to the recording later, you say, "Why is my voice so high? That's not how I sound." The difference can be very distracting, which is why you should get familiar with the sound of your voice.

When listening to your own voice as you're speaking, the sound vibrates through your skull, which lowers the frequency of vibration. It makes your voice sound lower and deeper.

When hearing your voice played back on a recording, you don't get the filter from your skull. That's why your voice sounds higher.

Admit it: This is the real voice others have been listening to when you talk.

Listen to your real voice more often. The more you listen to the recording, the more comfortable you'll feel about how you sound to others.

Speak Slower

Many speakers talk too fast without pausing – it's a sign that they feel nervous. When you feel confident and comfortable, you speak more slowly. When you speak slower, your voice becomes more powerful. The audience will be able to reflect on what you said. When you speak too quickly, the impact of your talk drops. People think what you're saying is less valuable.

Lose your "um" and "ah" with pauses

Most people say "um" and "ah" because they are uncomfortable with silence. The more nervous they feel, the more filler words they use.

Pause to show that you're confident. It also gives the audience time to digest what you said. You'll have more time to think about what to say next. You'll also get people's attention. Humans are hardwired to pay more attention during silence because they want to protect themselves from danger.

To avoid filler words, pause at the end of sentences. The audience will be able to digest what they learned.

Practice Projection

Speak loudly so that every person can hear you. Have enough energy to keep the audience's attention.

Imagine your good friend or family member is sitting in the back of the room (or ask one of them to sit at a distance from you) while you practice. Go through your talk speaking loud enough that your listener can hear you clearly.

Here is the actual physical process of practicing projection:

A. Breathe in through your nose

Most speakers breathe with their mouth. The cold air makes your throat and tongue feel very dry. Roger points out the importance of correct breathing, "If you want to control the sound, you have to learn to control the air."

We are born to breathe in through the nose. There are filters inside called turbinates. When air comes in through the nose, it becomes moist air, so when air goes to the throat and vocal chords, it won't dry them out.

Breathe in through your nose so you can stand up and speak for hours without feeling dry.

B. Pretend you have a balloon in your stomach

Most speakers hold their breath while doing public speaking. When you hold your breath, there's no air and your voice becomes weak.

Roger recommends filling your stomach with air, as though you had a balloon in there. Only speak while your stomach is coming in. "Every single person needs to breathe in through their nose, fill in their tummy as if the air was going in there, and then only speak while their stomach is coming in."

C. Warm up your voice

Just like athletes, great speakers do warm up exercises before performing. If they don't, their voice may get hurt. Do voice warm-up exercises.

One powerful exercise is called "goog": Regarding your pitch, start singing as low as you can, then go all up as high as you can, and then come back down. This gets the air going to the vocal cords and meet at the right spots, warming up your voice quickly.

Make sure you speak LOUDLY. You want everyone to hear you clearly.

What if your voice is very soft? People can't hear you clearly. What can you do?

When All Else Fails, Use a Microphone

Try to get a clip microphone if you can find one.

The handheld microphone locks your hands. You cannot move your hands freely and be yourself. Instead, use a clip microphone. Clip it on your collar so you can use your hands freely. The audience will also hear you clearly.

Ask the IT person for one.

No clip microphone? Don't worry. Any microphone is better than having no one hear what you have to say.

Change Your Speed

Once you learn how to pause, the next step is to vary your voice. Speak too fast, and your audience will think you're crazy. Speak too slowly, and you will bore people to sleep. The more you vary your voice, the more interesting your talk will be.

Changing your speed is a subtle way to hold your audience's attention. It works because humans are hardwired to identify changes. Keep your audience's attention by using contrasts. Only emphasise the important words and phrases. If you speak slowly and softly, emphasise a point by speaking quicker and louder. If you are a passionate speaker, highlight an important point by slowing down and lowering your voice. The key is to use contrast as a way of communicating what deserves the most attention. The audience will get your message more effectively.

When I deliver the message of my TEDx talk, I slow down and say, "How do we speak with confidence? Prepare, practice, perform."

In addition to pauses and contract, emphasise adjectives and adverbs to boost your energy and passion. You want the audience to hear and feel every word you say.

Let Emotions Be Your Guide

Speaking in a high pitch makes you sound nervous. To show you're confident, speak in a lower pitch at the end of a sentence. How do you vary the tone of your voice? Let the characters' emotions (happy, sad, angry) be your guide. If the character is sad, lower the voice. By expressing these emotions in the right tone, your voice will become more natural and powerful.

Record Your Voice And Get Feedback

Your voice is like a muscle. With exercise, it gets stronger. One of the best ways to strengthen your voice is to read a story out loud. Choose a short story that you love – it could be as brief as a few minutes– and record yourself in audio. Speak like you're in front of a live audience. When you read that story, put emotions and energy into the words.

Then listen to the recording and find areas for improvement. Ask yourself:

Is my voice loud enough?

Can I hear myself clearly?

Is my voice interesting?

Do I reflect the emotions that I feel?

Get feedback from a coach to make your voice more powerful.

Remember: the first time you listen to yourself, you may think your voice sounds weird. But the more you listen, the more comfortable you'll feel with it.

PRACTICING THE PROPER WAY: WHY PRACTICE DOESN'T MAKE PERFECT

When I was young and assigned to present a report to the class, my teacher told me "practice makes perfect." She was wrong. I practiced my talk in front of a mirror, trying to get over my fear of public speaking. But all I could see were red, angry pimples.

Then a "friend" told me to picture the audience in their underwear. As a teenager, I did it (of course). But this stupid idea made me feel even more uncomfortable. My mind went blank… I forgot what I was going to say… It was a disaster!

While I had spent a lot of time on practicing my report, I didn't realise that I could be practicing the wrong habits. If you're practicing the wrong habits, again and again, you're doomed to fail.

Here's Why Practice Doesn't Make Perfect

Over time, I realized that practice doesn't make perfect; practice with feedback makes great improvement.

So I paid tens of thousands of dollars to work with the best coaches, including TED speakers, world champions, and *New York Times* best-selling authors. We worked on my content, body language, and voice. That's how I discovered and developed most of the methods described in this book. One of my favourite techniques is The Simple Practice Method, which I've outlined below. You can use it to practice on your own and get awesome feedback.

Before we dive into it, however, I want to talk about a very important rule…

People, Please Stop Memorizing Word For Word

Memorizing every word of a speech is difficult and time-consuming – not to mention, it can be frustrating. If someone interrupts you, suddenly you will forget everything you wanted to say. Even if you can memorize word for word, you'll sound unnatural. There is a better way to remember what to say.

Only memorize your opening and closing. These two sections are what the audience will remember most. Also, lock in the main points and the structure of your stories. This may sound like terrible advice but let me tell you: If you memorize the whole speech or presentation, you will sound like a robot and be unnatural. Speak like a human, just like you're talking to friends, and your words will resonate more.

The Simple Practice Method – Improve Your Public Speaking Easily And Quickly

Video

You cannot give a talk and give yourself feedback at the same time.

Record yourself on video so that you can focus on giving the talk. Then relax and watch your performance as an audience member. That's how you give yourself quality feedback and improve your public speaking skills.

You don't need an expensive device. Just record yourself on video – even your phone's camera will do.

Feedback

It can be painful to watch yourself on video. Get over it. In order to put your recorded practices to work for you, you've got to assess your performance objectively. Worrying too much about what you don't like won't help; instead use the moments that make you embarrassed. What don't you like about them? What can you change?

I recommend you begin by focusing on your body language and the strength of your voice. Ask yourself:

Body language

- *Is my body language distracting?*

Are your hands shaking? Is the way you move your hands unnatural or uncomfortable? Are you moving your arms around too much? Too little? Are you moving on stage too much? Are you locked in one place? Mark that down and make sure you don't do that again.

If you are always moving, your movement will be meaningless. The audience will not know what's important. Move with a purpose.

Let the emotions in your story guide your movements. Feel the emotions and the body language will come naturally.

- *Do you look professional?*

Take the rehearsal seriously. Wear clothes that make you look great. You want to make the rehearsal as real as the actual talk. Remember, people judge you based on your look. Be the most well-dressed person in the room. You will feel more confident, and the audience will feel it too.

Voice

- *Can you hear yourself clearly?*

Volume matters. Make sure everybody can hear you clearly.

- *Do you pause after asking a rhetorical question?*

Ask a question and pause. Let people reflect on what you said.

- *Do you use "um" or "ah" a lot?*

If yes, then ask why. Do you need to practice that part of your talk more? Did you forget what you're going to say? Was your opening not strong enough? Were you nervous?

If you believe it's because you're moving through the talk too quickly, or your brain is working faster than your mouth, practice taking a pause here to gather your thoughts and start speaking again.

Feedback is one of the most powerful tools. Use it.

Focus

Focus on one area you did well. Keep doing that.

Then focus on one area for improvement. Concentrate on the one thing that troubles you during each round of practice.

Use The Simple Practice Method multiple times – first as a general assessment to figure out the areas that need improvement, and then in other rounds to address and fix problem areas.

Get More Feedback

While preparing for my TEDx talk, I practiced and asked for feedback. I went to TED speakers, Harvard professors, and million dollar speakers. One of the great pieces of advice I got was to use transitional phrases while moving on stage. Don't just move around because it's unnatural. Say, "Let's move on to point number two…" or, "Let's talk about point number three…"

This advice is worth every dollar I paid for it. I gave money and time. And I got even more money and valuable feedback.

Q&A AND IMPROMPTU SPEAKING: HOW TO ANSWER QUESTIONS LIKE A PRO

Great speakers are experts. By standing on stage and speaking about your topic, you will have authority because the audience sees you as an expert. But if you can't answer the audience's questions, you will lose that credibility.

I wanted to be an expert, so I learned how to answer questions like a pro. I can now think fast and have the answer to just about any question.

Please Read This Before You Have Another Q&A

If you end with the Q&A and you don't know how to answer a question, you'll look bad.

Have the Q&A before closing. Invite questions from the audience and answer them. People will appreciate you and follow your advice.

The Q&A Pro Formula – How To Think Fast And Have The Answer

Your best friend is now The Q&A Pro Formula, which consists of three steps:

Predict

The best way to answer questions is to predict them beforehand.

Write down any question that comes to mind while watching your recorded practices. Ask others to watch your talk and note down any questions that they have. If this is a speech that you'll be giving a few times, keep track of all questions that come up from your audience members.

When I was preparing for my TEDx talk on how to speak with confidence, I predicted these questions:

- Why do we fear public speaking?
- How can I remember what I want to say?
- What can I do to feel more comfortable speaking in public?

When I practiced the talk in front of other people, they gave me these additional questions:

- How to stop my voice from getting shaky?
- Is it true that the fear of public speaking never goes away?
- How can I grab people's attention?

When I delivered the talk in other venues before TEDx, I received these questions that I didn't expect:

- How many slides should I use in a presentation?
- How can I make my voice louder and stronger?
- How can I stop worrying about what others think and start speaking with confidence?

I save all of these questions and prepare my responses to them to make sure I'll always have the answer next time.

Invite questions

Set the expectation for how many questions you will answer. For example, you can say, "Before I close, I'll take three questions." By limiting the number of questions, you'll finish your talk on time.

Avoid asking, "Are there any questions?" because you may hear silence. Instead, ask, "What questions do you have?" This implies that audience members have questions, and will make them more likely to ask.

What if nobody asks a question? Prepare a common question you get and say, "One common question I get is…" Answer it quickly so you warm up the audience and get them prepared for questions. Then say, "We have time for two more questions. What questions do you have?"

Repeat

When people ask you a question, say, "So your question is…" and repeat it back to them.

Three benefits: You'll understand this question. You'll have more time to think. You'll give the right answer.

Answer

Answer the question effectively and concisely. Rambling will lose attention. This is where practice comes in. You don't want to bore others who don't care about the answer.

Get to the closing by saying, "Alright, we have gone through a lot today. Let's summarize what we have talked about…"

But what if someone asks me a question and I just don't know what to say?

Say, "That's a deep question. I need more time to think. I'll write a post for this group and answer this question. You can get the answer on my website or the organiser's website tomorrow."

Then move on to the next question or go directly to the closing.

Never assume that the one person asking is the only person interested in the question. Always give people a reason to connect with you, for example, by going to your website.

SPEAKING WITH CONFIDENCE: HOW TO FEEL COMFORTABLE SPEAKING IN PUBLIC

Just like top athletes and musicians, successful speakers have rituals before they perform. These rituals tell your brain, "It's time to deliver a talk."

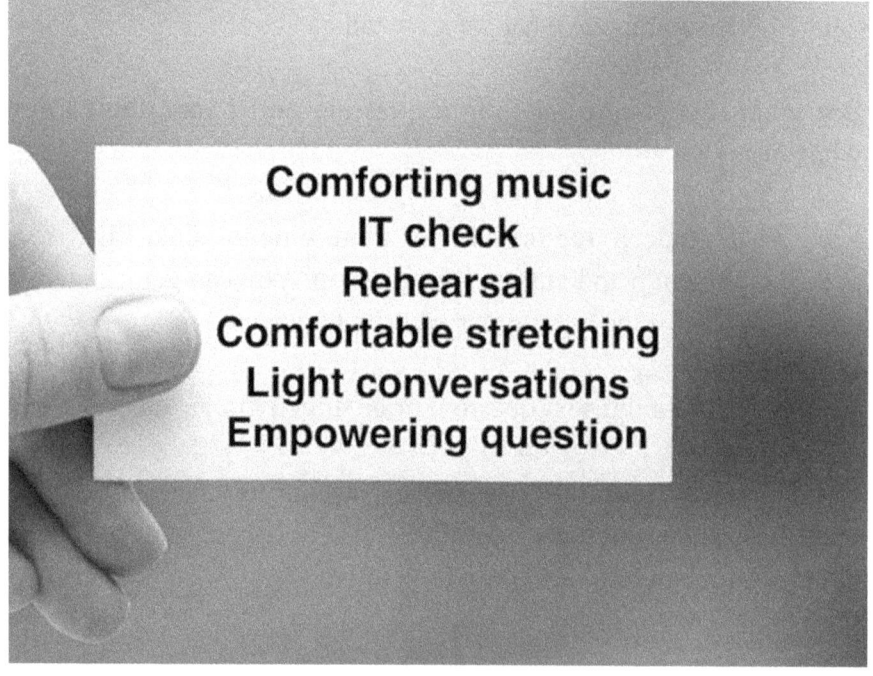

Create a Ritual That Will Bring You Success

Follow the steps below before you give a talk so it takes less work for your brain and your body responds automatically.

Comfortable music

On the way to the speaking venue, listen to music that makes you feel great. It boosts your energy while making you feel more relaxed and comfortable.

IT check

Arrive at the speaking venue early – say thirty minutes – so you can have more time to warm up.

Make sure your presentation slides run smoothly.

Check the microphone. Make sure everyone can hear you clearly.

If anything's wrong, contact the IT technician immediately.

Rehearsal

Walk around the room. Feel comfortable with the environment.

You don't have time to rehearse the entire talk. Just rehearse the opening. If you can deliver the opening confidently, the rest of your talk will also be great.

Say the opening out loud. If not possible, say it in your mind.

Comfortable stretching

Stretch your arms, legs, shoulders, and neck. Breathe. Relax your body.

Light conversations

Go back into the room. Go up to the audience members and say "Hi, my name is.... and I'm the speaker today."

When people see you talking to others in the group, they feel you care about them and will support you.

When giving the talk, look at those friendly people you spoke to earlier. Look at them as if you're having a one-on-one conversation. You'll feel more relaxed, calm, and in control.

Empowering question

Before delivering a talk, ask yourself, "What do I want the audience to think, feel or do *differently* after my talk?"

Remind yourself of the message and the benefits that it will bring to the audience. Put your focus on serving them. If you focus on serving the audience, the quality of your talk will go up, and your nervousness will go down.

Before going on stage, I focus on making people's lives better. It's not about you; it's about them. Get excited!

You do not have to follow these steps in the order listed. The idea is to create a public speaking success ritual to make you feel comfortable and confident. Put together a ritual that works best for you.

There's no better feeling than being comfortable and confident speaking in public.

Bye fear. Hi confidence.

CONCLUSION:
PUTTING IT ALL TOGETHER

The key to success is to become a confident public speaker. You will impress your boss, team, and clients.

So how do we speak with confidence? Here is a summary of the secrets to becoming a confident speaker. Review this list regularly until it becomes part of you, and you're guaranteed to succeed.

Prepare

A. Structure

- Create your message by asking "What do I want the audience to think, feel or do *differently* after my talk?" Pick three points that will support your message.

- Use a story to support each point. Make sure the audience can relate to your main character. Share a conflict to make your story interesting. Share the cure from an expert or a life-changing experience. Show how the solution has changed the main character's life.

- Open with a rhetorical question. Close with a short summary and clear call to action.

B. Slides

- Use sticky notes to sketch your ideas visually. One idea per slide. Fill each slide with a full image that creates a strong emotion.

Practice

A. Voice

- Lose your "um" and "ah" by pausing at the end of sentences. The audience will be able to digest what they learned.

- Fill your stomach with air, just like you had a balloon in there. Only speak while your stomach is coming in.

- Use a clip microphone so you can use your hands freely, and the audience will hear you clearly.

- Let the characters' emotions guide you. If you're making an important point, slow down and speak more softly. The audience will reflect on what you said.

- Record yourself reading a short story. Listen to the recording and find ways to improve your voice.

B. Video

- Practice doesn't make perfect, practice with feedback makes great improvement.

- Only remember your opening and closing because this is what the audience remembers the most. Also, remember the most important points and the structure of your stories.

- Record yourself giving the talk. Watch the video and focus on improving your body language and voice. Focus on one area for improvement.

C. Q&A

- Have the Q&A before closing. Invite questions from the audience and answer them. People will appreciate you and follow your advice.

- Write down any questions you may get during the talk. Set the expectation for how many questions you will answer. Repeat the question and answer it effectively and concisely.

- If you don't know the answer, offer to write a post and post the answer tomorrow.

Perform

- Before you deliver the talk, listen to music that makes you feel great.

- Arrive at the speaking venue early so you can check the technology and microphone.

- Rehearse the opening.

- Stretch and relax your body.

- Introduce yourself to audience members.

- Ask yourself, "What do I want the audience to think, feel or do *differently* after my talk?"

So What's Next?

Here's your next step: On my website, I've included a PDF that will remind you of the six steps of your Public Speaking Success Ritual.

To download it for free, go now to ImprovingPublicSpeaking.com/Resources.

Practice these techniques for your talks until they become part of you. With these secrets, you will become a confident public speaker.

Give your talk, share your message, and speak with confidence.

ABOUT THE AUTHOR

Jonathan Li is a successful public speaking coach, movie lover, and writer. He has given dozens of talks, including a TEDx talk on how to speak with confidence.

His writing appears in major media outlets, including *The Huffington Post, Lifehack, Business Insider*, and others. He has attracted more than 300,000 views.

Jonathan is the author of five books. Join him and receive free resources at ImprovingPublicSpeaking.com.